Animals in my Backyard

RACCOONS

Jordan McGill

www.av2books.com

Go to www.av2books.com, and enter this book's unique code.

BOOK CODE

Z648913

AV² by Weigl brings you media enhanced books that support active learning.

AV² provides enriched content that supplements and complements this book. Weigl's AV² books strive to create inspired learning and engage young minds in a total learning experience.

Your AV² Media Enhanced books come alive with...

Audio
Listen to sections of the book read aloud.

Video
Watch informative video clips.

Embedded Weblinks
Gain additional information for research.

Try This!
Complete activities and hands-on experiments.

Key Words
Study vocabulary, and complete a matching word activity.

Quizzes
Test your knowledge.

Slide Show
View images and captions, and prepare a presentation.

... and much, much more!

Published by AV² by Weigl
350 5th Avenue, 59th Floor New York, NY 10118
Website: www.av2books.com www.weigl.com

Library of Congress Cataloging-in-Publication Data

McGill, Jordan.
Raccoons / Jordan McGill.
p. cm. -- (Animals in my backyard)
ISBN 978-1-61690-932-1 (hardcover : alk. paper) -- ISBN 978-1-61690-578-1 (online)
1. Raccoon--Juvenile literature. I. Title.
QL737.C26M43 2012
599.76'32--dc23
2011023436

Printed in the United States of America in North Mankato, Minnesota
1 2 3 4 5 6 7 8 9 0 15 14 13 12 11

062011
WEP030611

Project Coordinator: Jordan McGill Art Director: Terry Paulhus

Weigl acknowledges Getty Images as the primary image supplier for this title.

Animals in my Backyard

RACCOONS

CONTENTS

Meet the raccoon.

She looks like she wears a mask.

She lives with her family.

With her family,
she travels and climbs.

She moves from one home to another.

From one home to another,
she looks for food.

She takes food with little hands.

Little hands help her eat animals and plants.

She can climb head first
up and down, high up in trees.

High up in trees,
she is not afraid of falling.

She has rings on her fluffy, striped tail.

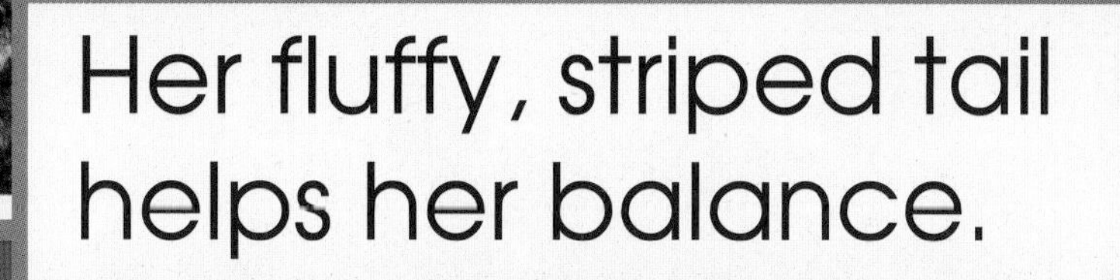

Her fluffy, striped tail
helps her balance.

During the day,
she is in hiding.

In hiding,
she waits for night.

She can live near people.

Near people, she finds food in garbage cans.

If you meet the raccoon,
she may look small and cute.
She is fierce.

If you meet the raccoon,
stay away.

RACCOON FACTS

This page provides more detail about the interesting facts found in the book. Simply look for the corresponding page number to match the fact.

Pages 4-5

Raccoons have dark fur around their eyes that looks like a mask. Raccoons have a pointed snout and a bushy, ringed tail. They have gray or brown fur on their body. Adult raccoons can grow to be 3 feet (0.9 meters) long. Most raccoons weigh up to 40 pounds (18 kilograms). Female raccoons are usually smaller than males.

Pages 6–7

At about one month of age, a baby raccoon, or cub, can stand. When cubs are two to three months old, they begin to hunt with their mother. She protects them from predators. Most raccoons stay with their mother for up to one year. A female raccoon may stay with their litter until she has another litter. Males live alone. They do not help raise the babies.

Pages 8–9

Raccoons move to a new living space in their territory every few days. They travel to find food. Raccoons stay in one place during the winter. The cold forces them to keep warm in their dens. Most raccoons move into dens that other animals have abandoned.

Pages 10–11

Raccoons are omnivores. They eat insects, birds, eggs, fish, and small rabbits with their paws. They also eat fruits and vegetables, such as plums and corn. A raccoon's paws are almost like hands. Raccoons can spread their toes to grab food and other objects. They can grab fish out of the water and overturn rocks with their paws.

Pages 12–13

Raccoons are excellent climbers. They are one of the few animals that can climb down trees head first. They do this by turning their hind feet so that their toes face backwards. Raccoons have little fear when they are high in trees. A raccoon can drop more than 40 feet (12 m) without getting hurt.

Pages 14–15

A raccoon's tail fur usually has five to seven dark circles. Raccoon tails can be more than 10 inches (25 centimeters) long. Raccoons use their tail for balance when they are climbing.

Pages 16–17

Raccoons are mostly nocturnal. This means they are most active at night. During the day, they stay in trees or hide under rocks, underground, or in buildings. Raccoons see well at night. They prefer to look for food in the dark. The dark mask of fur around their eyes may help them see better at night. It helps reduce the glare of the Sun and the Moon.

Pages 18–19

Raccoons are very smart. Some raccoons can open garbage cans, latches, and even jars. Raccoons have learned that they can find food near people. They are often found searching through garbage at night. People can teach raccoons to stay away by keeping their garbage clean and secure.

Pages 20–21

Sometimes, raccoons live near people. If a raccoon lives near you, do not feed it. Raccoons can be dangerous. They are strong for their size and have sharp claws. Raccoons fight when they feel threatened, and they can carry diseases. If a raccoon is outside your house, turn on lights to drive it away. Raccoons prefer the dark.

WORD LIST

Research has shown that as much as 65 percent of all written material published in English is made up of 300 words. These 300 words cannot be taught using pictures or learned by sounding them out. They must be recognized by sight. This book contains 47 common sight words to help young readers improve their reading fluency and comprehension. This book also teaches young readers several important content words. These words are paired with pictures to aid in learning and improve understanding.

Page	Sight Words First Appearance
4	the
5	a, like, looks, she
6	and, family, her, lives, with
8	another, from, home, moves, one, to
9	food, for
10	hands, little, takes
11	animals, eat, help, plants
12	can, down, first, head, high, in, trees, up
13	is, no, of
14	has, on
16	day, night
18	near, people
19	finds
21	away, but, may, small

Page	Content Words First Appearance
4	raccoon
5	mask
14	rings, tail
19	cans, garbage